W9-AHY-594

J
796.7
Ste
Stewart
Motorcycle racing

R436699
10.95

DATE DUE		
AG 14 '89		
JY 02 '90		
OC 18 '91		
JY 13 '92		
MY 24 '93		
SE 03 '93		
NO 14 '94		
MR 30 '95		
DE 17 '95		

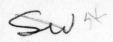

GREAT RIVER REGIONAL LIBRARY

St. Cloud, Minnesota   56301

SUPER-CHARGED!

MOTORCYCLE RACING

BY

Gail Stewart

PUBLISHED BY

CRESTWOOD HOUSE

Mankato, MN, U.S.A.

2851616

CIP

LIBRARY OF CONGRESS CATALOGING IN PUBLICATION DATA

Stewart, Gail
  Motorcycle racing.
  (Super-charged!)
  Includes index.
  SUMMARY: Discusses different motorcycle races such as speedway, road, BMX, and hillclimbing racing and describes the variety of cycles used in them.
  1. Motorcycle racing—Juvenile literature. [Motorcycle racing] I. Title
GV1060.S79   1988   796.7'5   87-33198
ISBN 0-89686-360-3

International Standard	**Library of Congress**
Book Number:	**Catalog Card Number:**
0-89686-360-3	87-33198

CREDITS

Cover: Focus West: (David Klutho)
CJS Racing: (Carol Steimer Bailey) 9, 10-11
Journalism Services: 22, 23
Third Coast Stock Source: (Lawrence Ruggeri) 28-29; (John M. Touscany) 32;
  (Todd V. Phillips) 33
FPG International: 17; (Thomas Zimmerman) 4, 7, 12, 16; (Ron Whitby) 18
Focus West: (David Klutho) 14-15; (James Perez) 20-21, 43; (Brian Geddis) 25, 31, 40;
  (Bob Grieser) 26-27; (Larry Prosor) 35, 36; (Robert Beck) 39
SIPPA Sports/Focus West: 19

Copyright ©1988 by Crestwood House, Inc. All rights reserved. No part of this book may be reproduced in any form without written permission from the publisher, except for brief passages included in a review. Printed in the United States of America.

Produced by Carnival Enterprises.

CRESTWOOD HOUSE

Box 3427, Mankato, MN, U.S.A. 56002

TABLE OF CONTENTS

The Race is On!.................................. 5
Beginnings 5
A Sport Apart 7
Speedway Racing 8
But No Brakes 12
Daytona 200.....................................16
Road Racing Cycles 18
Sidecar Racing.................................22
Motocross 24
Motocross Bikes................................30
You Want to Dump That Dirt Where?...........33
Observed Trials 34
SSHHHHHH!.......................................37
Walking the Traps 37
Trials Cycles 38
For the Fun Of It..............................39
Hillclimb Racing 41
Hillclimbing Machines.........................42
Hillclimbing Challenges 44
For the Love Of It.............................45
Glossary/Index 46-47

R 436699

The beginning of another motorcycle race.

THE RACE IS ON!

It's a hazy August afternoon. In less than a minute the green flag will go up, starting one of the biggest motorcycle races of the year. Thousands of people have jammed the stadium bleachers. They watch you and the other racers as you ease your motorcycle up to the starting line. Sleek and streamlined, your cycle glistens in the sunshine.

You take a quick sideways look at the racers to your left. There are powerful racing machines—Harleys, Yamahas, Kawasakis. The other riders are looking straight ahead. Are they feeling as nervous and excited as you are?

Your hand twists the throttle and your engine buzzes and whines. All of the motorcycles are revving louder and louder. The crowd roars. The green flag is up! The motorcycles lurch forward in a big noisy swarm. The race is on!

BEGINNINGS

There is no record of the first motorcycle race. It's a sure bet, though, that riders began to get together to test the speed of their machines back in 1885, when the motorcycle was invented.

The first motorcycles were really bicycles, with small gasoline engines mounted under the seats. They weren't very sturdy, since they had no shock absorbers (shock absorbers make the motorbike ride smoothly, even on bumps). Those first motorcycles were pretty slow — but that made sense. Even the best roads back then were rutted and terribly bumpy. And since gas stations didn't exist, it was pretty hard to get gas for your motorbike!

By the early 1900's, many companies were making motorcycles. The large American companies were Harley-Davidson, Indian, Royal, and Mitchell. Each company wanted to sell more than the other, so they all tried to make their motorcycles easier to ride. Gas tanks got bigger, shock absorbers got much better, and seats became softer.

These motorcycle companies knew that Americans loved speed. A good way to show just how fast their cycles could go was to run in public races. The companies hired daring young riders who weren't afraid to go at top speed. By 1910 some of the faster motorcycles could go almost 60 miles per hour (mph) or 96 kilometers per hour (km/h).

Oval-shaped dirt tracks were perfect for racing, so motorcycle events were held on horse race tracks at county fairgrounds. These races, and the daredevils who rode in them, attracted huge crowds all over the country.

A motorcyclist needs good balance — especially around the turns.

A SPORT APART

Since those early days, motorcycle racing has become one of the fastest growing sports in the world. There is no other sport quite like it.

Both driver and machine must be in top condition. Many motorcycles weigh as much as 600 pounds (270 kilograms). To steer one of these large machines

around tight turns on a slippery dirt track, or to perform hair-raising jumps on a cross-country course requires strength and balance. A rider must be an athlete, or his chances of finishing a race are very slight.

Another reason motorcycle racing is so different from other sports is its "path to the top." In baseball, the best team is the winner of the World Series. In pro football, it's the Super Bowl champion. But in professional motorcycle racing, it's not just the winner of one event—it can be as many as 30! These events are called the Grand National Championship Series (GNC). Even more unusual, the GNC champ has to be a winner in several different kinds of motorcycle races.

It seems there are as many kinds of motorcycle races as there are motorcycles!

SPEEDWAY RACING

Speedway racing is just what its name suggests— fast! Thousands of people come to watch the fastest motorcycle races of them all.

Speedway races are held on oval tracks. Usually the surfaces of these tracks are made of dirt or cinders. But other surfaces, like grass or cement, are used, too. There are even some speedway tracks in Sweden and Russia that have ice surfaces! Motorcycles racing on

The green light means Go!

ice must be equipped with special tires with spikes on them. This helps the cycle get traction on the slick, dangerous surface.

Just before World War I, some people thought it would be fun to have speedway races indoors. That way, officials would not have to cancel a race because

A motorcyclist waits for his turn to race.

of bad weather. These indoor tracks were called "velodromes" or "motordromes." Indoor racing proved to be a bad idea, however. The wooden boards used for the track surface were slippery. Oil from the motorcycles made the track even slicker. Many riders

were hurt—some were even killed. Speedway racing
went back outdoors.

Today, most speedway races in the United States are
held on dirt ovals. The sport has come to be called
"flat-track racing."

All motorcyclists wear protective clothing and helmets.

BUT NO BRAKES

"Simple" is the best word for the speedway motorcycle. It has a frame, wheels, and an engine. There is no starter. Racers start their machines by pushing them. But the most surprising thing about speedway cycles is that they have no brakes! The key to speedway racing is acceleration (gaining speed) so there isn't much point in slowing down during a race.

The tricky spots, of course, are the curves in the track. How does a rider turn his cycle without slowing down? The rider goes through his turns in a slide. This is called "broadsiding." When a racer comes to a turn, he leans into the turn, steers away from it, and plants his foot down on the track. This helps him keep his balance (usually!) without losing valuable time on the clock. Speedway racers wear special boots with steel caps on the toes and hard metal soles. This protects their feet when they "hot shoe" around the turns.

The speedway race always moves in a counterclockwise direction. Four racers compete at one time. They start behind a set of tapes which stretch across the track. Sometimes a rider is too eager to start and breaks one of the tapes before the race begins. If that happens, he is excluded from the race. When the green flag is waved, the race starts.

During the course of the race, other flags are used. Flags are important because they give information to riders and spectators. An official waves a black flag when a rule has been broken and a rider has been disqualified. A yellow flag with a black cross on it tells the riders that there is only one lap to go (usually, a race is four laps around the track). A red flag means that the race has been stopped for some reason—an accident, maybe, or bad weather. And the black-and-white checkered flag signals the end of the speedway race—and a winner has crossed the finish line!

Motorcyclists use their feet to make turns without falling.

DAYTONA 200

The most famous racetrack in the United States is the Daytona International Speedway in Daytona Beach, Florida. The Daytona 200 race is held every March. It is a dangerous, high-speed event.

Tens of thousands of motorcyclists from all over the world arrive in Daytona Beach each spring. Some have come to race, but many just come to have a good time watching. Unlike most speedway events, this race

The racetrack at the Daytona 200 is a hard asphalt surface.

Motorcyclists need quick reflexes to avoid an accident on the racetrack.

takes place on a hard asphalt surface—just like a highway. And because the course is much longer than on an oval track, very high speeds are reached. Sometimes riders will go more than 160 mph (260 km/h) on the Daytona straightaway!

But speed alone won't win this 200-mile (320-kilometer) race. The course winds around and around. A wide, four-lane straightaway can suddenly shrink to a narrow little alley where racers are only inches apart. Good judgment and quick reflexes are a must at Daytona.

Road racing cycles are streamlined to help them go as fast as they can.

ROAD RACING CYCLES

In the motorcycle world, road racing cycles are the beauties. They are sleek, shiny, and colorful. Somehow they just *look* fast!

Streamlining is what gives these bikes their fast appearance. To streamline a bike, a motorcycle designer covers the body of the bike with a special case, called a "fairing." The fairing is rounded and tapered. This design lets the air flow past the

18

motorcycle without slowing it down. Without fairings, a racing bike can go about 100 mph (160 km/h). That same bike, with fairings, can sometimes reach speeds of 195 mph (313 km/h)!

There are a few other adjustments a rider or his

During a race, a motorcyclist is faced with many challenges.

For the best performance, slicks, instead of tread tires, are used on road racing cycles.

mechanic might make on a road racer. The first is to increase the size of the cylinders in the engine. Bigger cylinders can help the engine put out more power.

Another way to make a road racing bike even faster is to change the type of tires used. Normal tires have

"treads," which are raised patterns that give the bike traction. The road racing bike uses smooth tires without tread. These tires are called "slicks." On a speedway surface like asphalt or cement, slicks help the road racing cycle go very fast.

SIDECAR RACING

Sidecar racing is one of the most fun-to-watch events at the track. A sidecar machine, or "hack," as it is sometimes called, is very low and streamlined. There is a flat platform on the side. The platform is

In sidecar racing, the passenger works harder than the driver!

It takes courage and skill to be a monkey on a sidecar.

where the driver's passenger sits. The whole vehicle looks a little bit like a three-wheeled car.

A passenger is usually someone who is just along for the ride—not so with sidecar passengers! A sidecar passenger works harder than the driver. His job is to balance the motorcycle, especially when it is hurtling around corners at top speed. Often he will have to climb up, down, or perch on top of the driver to keep the whole rig from tipping over. No wonder this passenger is called a "monkey." Sometimes the monkey must hang so far out of the sidecar that the seat of his pants almost scrapes the track.

Other drivers look at sidecar racers and monkeys with a mixture of respect and amazement. They admire the courage and talent it takes to race sidecar-style. But wild, high-speed rides an inch over the track make the other racers shake their heads. "You've got to be nuts!" they say.

MOTOCROSS

Another kind of motorcycle racing is called "motocross" or "MX." Motocross events are run on an enclosed track—usually between one and one-and-one-half miles (about two kilometers) long. But this track is far different than the one used in flat-track racing.

An MX track is an obstacle course for motorcycles. There are hills, jumps, water, mud, and plenty of turns—both left and right. There are short straight-aways, bone-jarring bumps called "whoop-de-dos," and anything else the organizers of the event can think of!

The object of a motocross race is to complete as many laps around the track as you possibly can in a given number of minutes. Riders have two time periods, or "motos," to go through their paces. That's where the name of the sport comes from. A moto can be 15, 20, 30, or 40 minutes long, depending on the

An MX motorcyclist tackles a whoop-de-doo.

A motorcross event always attracts many racers.

ability of the group.

The rider who does the most laps in a moto gets one point. The number two rider gets two points, and so on. The rider with the lowest number of points after two motos is declared the winner.

At the start of a motocross race, the riders line up at a starting gate, much like the ones used in horse races. There are usually 40 racers competing at the same time. When the gate drops, 40 motorcycles zoom into the first turn. Within a matter of seconds, the pack

Motorcross racers know how to kick-up the dust.

will be going 50 mph (80 km/h). Cinders, mud, sand, and water fly as 80 wheels tear up the course. Experienced motocross racers know that it's no fun being in the rear of the group. So much mud flies

around that it is very hard to see anything.

Also, in a group of racers going 30-50 mph (48-80 km/h), it's important to be very alert. It is very easy to slide into another racer on a turn and risk injuries.

But no matter how wide-awake MX racers are, there will be spills and slides. That's just the nature of the sport. For fans and riders alike, that's part of the excitement!

MOTOCROSS BIKES

Motocross motorcycles must be extremely light and easy to control. That is very important. The suspension system of the bike has to be good. Experienced MX racers almost always make adjustments on the suspension before a race. The condition of the track will determine how tight or how loose the suspension should be.

The tires of MX bikes are called "knobbies." They have raised bumps to help the tires grip on sand and other loose surfaces.

Many of the motorcycle companies that make the best motocross machines have also begun making "mini" MX motorcycles. There has been a big demand for these junior cycles, especially in the United States. Boys and girls aged five and up are taking part in junior MX events around the country.

Motocross is a tough sport. It is hard on motorcycles and riders. But there are more motocross racers in the United States than any other racing group on two wheels!

An MX bike's "knobbies" supply traction—but can't help much in mid-air!

Concentration is needed when riding the "snake pits."

Spills are bound to happen.

YOU WANT TO DUMP THAT DIRT WHERE?

Motocross racing has been getting very popular for fans as well as for riders. Crowds love to watch MX racers battling the jumps and gullies, which are often called "snake pits." And it's so much fun watching people get really dirty! For those reasons, there are more and more MX races every year in Europe and in the United States. Sometimes over 50,000 people come to watch an event. Often the races are televised.

Motocross racing has another location—indoors! Not long ago, a parade of huge dump trucks hauling black dirt and sand drove into the Superdome in New Orleans. Many thousands of tons of dirt were needed to create an indoor MX course. The track was set up— a tough one with lots of bumps and whoop-de-dos— and even larger crowds than expected came to cheer on the racers.

OBSERVED TRIALS

In the famous story about the tortoise and the hare, the moral was "slow and steady wins the race." This is the idea behind a motorcycle contest called Observed Trials.

It makes no difference how slow or how fast a Trials rider goes. What is important is how well he can handle his machine in almost impossible conditions. What are these conditions? The "trials" in a Trials course can be hills, fallen logs, rivers, streams, or large rocks. And if the course doesn't look hard enough, the race officials may add a few hazards of their own!

There are anywhere from 10 to 20 trials in an event. These trials, or "traps" as they are sometimes called, are marked with poles and rope. Two red flags tell the racer that a trap is beginning. Two green flags mark the end of each trap.

A large rock is just one of the obstacles a cyclist faces on an observed trials course.

Observed trials courses are carefully marked—but they don't look easy.

SSHHHHHH!

On the Observed Trials course, judges stand near each trap. They watch the riders carefully. Each rider begins with a score of 1,000 points. If a rider leans against something to keep his balance, that will cost him points. He loses a point every time he puts his foot on the ground for balance. This is called a "dab." It's very hard to complete a trap without using the feet for balance, especially with so many obstacles in the way. There is a large penalty for leaving a trap section before finishing it. Five points is the penalty for straying outside the trap borders.

Doing a trap "clean" means finishing without breaking any rules. For a clean trap, a rider scores zero points. And that's hard to do!

Besides the judges, there are usually spectators standing alongside the traps. Spectators must be perfectly quiet when a rider is going through a trap. That's so the rider can concentrate every inch of the way. Everyone claps for a rider when he finally reaches the green flags at the end of each trap.

WALKING THE TRAPS

Good riders want to look over the Trials course before the event starts. That is a smart thing to do. No one likes to be surprised by loose gravel or a bed of mud in the middle of a contest!

When the riders make their inspections, they park their bikes and walk. It is easier to check for trouble spots on foot. What kind of things do they look for? Since most Observed Trials have a stream or creek to cross, it's a good idea to walk through the water. That way a rider can see how deep the stream is. He can also tell if there are any big stones at the bottom that might be a problem for his tires.

TRIALS CYCLES

The motorcycles used in Trials events are quite different from bikes used in other contests. Since these riders stand almost the whole time, the handlebars are set higher and the bikes have special pegs (pegs are the footrests on a motorcycle). They are set back, close to the rear wheel. This way a rider can lean way back to do rear-wheel balancing, or "wheelies," over logs and rocks.

A good Trials cycle is light. Often these motorcycles weigh only 200 pounds (90 kilograms). Despite their trim weight, the frames of these bikes must be very strong.

Racing bikes have names most people recognize— Yamaha, Kawasaki, Honda. But Trials bikes have more unfamiliar names like Ossa, Butalco, and Montessa. These motorcycles are all built in Spain.

The crowd cheers on another racer.

FOR THE FUN OF IT

Observed Trials riding sounds very difficult, and it is. But there's none of the breakneck speed of flat-track or road racing. In fact, Trials riding is the safest of all motorcycle sports.

Since the Trials bikes are all pretty much alike, Trials are more of a human contest than a mechanical one. In speedway racing, the motorcycles themselves are often the "stars"—the best rider in the world can't

The love of racing keeps most motorcyclists happy.

win unless he's got the best machine. But in Trials, it's rider against rider. As one experienced Trials rider put it, "If *you* don't have it, your bike can't help you at all!"

Although Observed Trials is a very tough sport, experts say that it's the best way to really learn to ride a motorcycle. You can learn more about balance in an afternoon of Trials, they say, than in 20 years of regular road riding. That must be true. Riders go very slowly, sometimes barely moving at all. Just as with riding a bicycle, speed can be a great balancer. The minute you slow down, though, your bike is a lot more wobbly. It's harder to stay upright.

On a motorcycle, riders experience the same feeling. Since they are moving at about the same speed as a tortoise, they need to use their bodies to balance. Most of the time, riders will be standing on the pegs as they climb over boulders or creep along logs thrown across deep rivers.

HILLCLIMB RACING

Hillclimb racing is really two different sports. In one, the object is to go faster than anyone else up the side of a steep hill. The second type is a contest of distance—who can go farthest up a hill. Both kinds of hillclimbing can be wild.

Like Motocross or Observed Trials events, racers will find rugged surfaces going up a hill. There are rocks, sand, bumps, and gravel.

In a timed event, racers don't have to go all the way to the top of the hill. As soon as the green flag is waved, one racer makes a mad dash up the side of the hill. The official carefully times him with a stopwatch. When each rider has made a run, the one with the fastest time is declared the winner.

In a hillclimb distance competition, two riders go at the same time. The riders travel as far as they can before they lose control, or come to a complete standstill. If a rider puts his foot on the ground, or falls backward, officials mark that spot. All riders get three turns. The one with the mark closest to the top of the hill is the winner.

HILLCLIMBING MACHINES

To reach the top of the hill, bikers must get a fast start. The bikers build up speed while they can, because as the hill gets steeper, the going gets slower.

A rider wants a motorcycle with lots of accelerating power. It must also be lightweight. Anything that isn't absolutely necessary is stripped off the bike. A rider doesn't want to drag any extra weight up a hill.

When a cycle is climbing a steep slope, the front end will sometimes pop up, or "wheelie," in the air. While wheelies are important in Observed Trials and MX races, they can be dangerous on a steep hill. For this reason, riders move the engines of their bikes forward, toward the front wheel. This helps keep the front end down.

Some big, expensive, top-level machines even use special fuel for extra power. Mixed in with the gasoline is a gas called nitrous oxide. Nitrous oxide helps the gasoline by giving it a "boost." The mixture burns hotter and cleaner than ordinary gasoline. This increases the horsepower of the engine. This fuel can be dangerous, though, because it's very flammable. But biking experts take the risk, because the extra horsepower they get might just get them all the way to the top of the hill!

Motorcycle racers love speed!

HILLCLIMBING CHALLENGES

With all the potential hazards of hillclimbing, there are many precautions a racer must take.

During the climb, a racer has to stay bent over so there is weight on both wheels. His backside presses on the rear wheel, while he leans forward and presses down on the front wheel with the handlebars. This takes great arm strength.

Many racers lose control as the "incline," or angle of the hill, becomes steeper. It's very important to know how to get off the motorcycle fast. One of the rules at a hillclimb event is that every cycle has a "deadman's switch." This switch turns the engine off when the rider falls off (or jumps off) his bike. It's switched off by a bracelet the rider wears that is attached to the ignition of the cycle. When the rider falls off, the bracelet jerks. This sudden jerk stops the engine. But even with the deadman's switch, a rider must get out of the way of his cycle before it falls back on him.

The danger of any hillclimbing event depends a lot on the hill. One of the most famous event hills is called Widowmaker Hill in Utah. The terrain is terrible, filled with sharp, loose rocks and sand. Widowmaker Hill was even featured in a movie about hillclimb racing called *On Any Sunday.* Mount Garfield in

Michigan is another famous hill that has been tormenting riders for many years. Big John Hill in California has dangerous inclines to climb, some as steep as 70 degrees!

FOR THE LOVE OF IT

If you asked most motorcycle racers why they do what they do—why race sidecar, or Observed Trials, or MX, or any of the other kinds of racing events—they probably wouldn't be able to tell you. It certainly isn't for the prize money. Even the most important motorcycle events offer small cash prizes compared to other sports. Besides, most riders are amateurs, which means they race for the love of the sport and not for money.

The satisfaction and pride a rider feels when he or she has done better than all the others is the best prize of all!

GLOSSARY/INDEX

BROADSIDING 13 — *To lean into a turn while using the foot to keep the motorcycle balanced.*

CLEAN 37 — *Finishing an Observed Trials event without breaking any rules.*

DAB 37 — *Using the feet to balance a motorcycle during an Observed Trials event.*

DEADMAN'S SWITCH 44 — *This switch automatically turns the engine off when a rider falls or jumps off his motorcycle.*

FAIRING 18, 19 — *The casing or shell that streamlines a road racing cycle.*

FLAT-TRACK RACING 11, 24, 39 — *Another name for Speedway racing.*

HACK 22 — *A sidecar machine that includes a flat platform designed for a passenger.*

HILLCLIMB RACING 41, 42, 44 — *A race to the top of a steep hill.*

HORSEPOWER 43 — *The unit for measuring the power of an engine.*

KNOBBIES 30 — *Tires especially made for MX bikes. Knobbies have raised bumps to grip sand and gravel.*

MONKEY 23, 24 — *Nickname for the passenger of a sidecar machine.*

MOTO 24, 26 — *One time period in a motocross race.*

MOTOCROSS 24, 27, 28, 30, 33, 34, 41 — *Cross-country motorcycle racing; also known as MX.*

OBSERVED TRIALS 34, 37, 38, 39, 41, 42, 45 —

GLOSSARY/INDEX

A motorcycle contest that challenges the biker to maneuver through and around obstacles including fallen logs, streams, and large rocks.

PEGS 38, 41 — *The footrests on a motorcycle.*

SHOCK ABSORBERS 6 — *A device on a vehicle that absorbs the forces of road shocks. Shock absorbers allow motorcyclists to have a smoother ride, even when they are driving over rocky trails.*

SLICKS 21 — *Tires without treads made for road racing cycles.*

SNAKE PIT 33 — *The gullies that bikers must drive through in motocross racing.*

SPEEDWAY RACING 8 — *A race around an oval track.*

STREAMLINE 5 — *To design a vehicle with a special shell that allows the airflow to pass around the vehicle without slowing it down.*

TRAPS 34, 37 — *The obstacles facing a biker in an Observed Trials event.*

TREADS 21 — *Raised patterns on tires that give the vehicle traction.*

VELODROME 10 — *An indoor, oval-shaped racetrack.*

WHEELIES 38, 42 — *A maneuver in which the driver raises the front wheel of a motorcycle or bicycle so that it is balanced on its rear wheel.*

WHOOP-DE-DO 24 — *Short straightaways in a motocross race filled with bone-jarring bumps.*